This Book Belongs To:

____

9 781796 321661